My True Invisible Friend

Mary Perry

Absolute Author Publishing House, New Orleans, LA

Absolute Author
Publishing House

My True Invisible Friend
Copyright ©2020
Mary Perry

Scripture quotations marked NLT are from the Holy Bible: New Living Translation. 1997 by Tyndale House Publishers, Inc. Wheaton, Illinois. USED WITH PERMISSION.

Scripture quotations marked KJV are from the Holy Bible: The Original King James Version. 1985 by Dugan Publishers, Inc. Gordonsville, Tennessee 38563. USED WITH PERMISSION.

Publisher's Cataloging-in-Publication Data
Editor: Dr. Melissa Caudle
Cover Designer: Xee_Designs1

Mary Perry/*My True Invisible Friend*
My Ture Invisible Friend/Perry, Mary
    p. cm.

ISBN: 978-1-951028-90-9

    1.   Memoir 2. Spiritual 3. Religious 4. Self-help

DEDICATION

To my family, may they always receive His blessings from upon high. To God be the Glory in all things.

Table of Contents

Food Poisoning   1

Falling in Love with an Invisible Friend   3

Jesus, the True Vine   5

My Invisible Friend   10

and the Rottweiler Dog   10

My Invisible Friend and the Poisonous Snake   12

My Invisible Friend and the Anesthesia Drugs   15

A Battle with Cancer   17

My Invisible Friend Reaching Out to Help Others   18

My Invisible Friend at Six Flags Over Texas   19

How My Coworker Met My Invisible Friend   21

My Invisible Friend is Concerned About the Little
Things in Life   23

My Invisible Friend Spared My Brother's Life   25

A Trip to the Zoo   26

A Bomb   28

A Teaching Position   29

Meeting My Husband   31

Prayer Changes Things   35

Riding Home   37

My Twin Sister   39

My Best Friend   43

Never Give Up on Your Child   45

My Economics Class   48

Meeting My Invisible Friend   50

   Jesus, the True Vine   51

About the Author   56

Resources   57

Food Poisoning

On May 12, 2020, approximately about 6:20 p.m., during the COVID-19 Pandemic. I believe it was food poisoning because I was feeling good until I ate my dinner. Well, later, my body was in excruciating pain on a ten plus Richter scale. The pain grew more intense; the longer I fought it. I knew I should call 911 and have an ambulance transport me to the emergency room, but then I thought about the wait time and process. Did I really want to do that and take the risk of COVID-19 exposure?

The second thought to call Pastor Duncan seemed more logical because she is an anointed intercessor ordained and created by God. I called her immediately and explained that I was in severe pain, and she delivered a prayer of **intercession on** my behalf. Within a few minutes, I felt a touch from my invisible friend. I started feeling better because of what the Lord had done through his mighty power and the word of God. Some of the scriptures, that were used which included the following.

Psalm 91: 15-16 - *He shall call upon me, and I will answer him: I will be with him in trouble; I will deliver him and honour him. With long life will I satisfy him and shew him my salvation.*

Psalm 118:17 - *I shall not die, but live and declare the works of the Lord.*

Proverbs 18:21 - *Death and life are in the power of the tongue: and they that love it shall eat the fruit thereof.*

Jeremiah 1:12 - *I am watching over My word to perform it.*

Hebrews 13:8 - *Jesus Christ the same yesterday, and today, and forever and the list continued. I know one thing that I was delighted to be feeling better. I had to praise and thank God for the miracle he performed in my body.*

Falling in Love with an Invisible Friend

One day I planned a trip to Richmond, California, to visit my second oldest brother. I wanted to see him so we could go out and have a wonderful time in the clubs, visiting relatives and friends. Once I made the reservation to fly to California, I noticed that something strange was taking place in my body, and it was not good. I was in my private bedroom, where I lived with a family from New Orleans, Louisiana. I had to think really fast on my feet, as the changes were taking place more rapidly than I cared to admit.

I tried calling for help, but I had no voice, I noticed that my strength was leaving my body amazingly fast, and I was falling on the floor. I tried to prevent the fall and wanted to pull myself up so

I could rest on the bed, but I had no strength in my physical body. I laid on the floor, and I could not move my body. I started talking to God in my mind because he was finished with my lying mouth (not telling the truth). He brought it back to my attention that I had promised to go and spend some time with my younger sister, Arquillia.

At that particular time, I told my sister a lie that I was coming to visit her, but I had no intention to carry it out. I told her that so she could stop asking me about visiting her in Birmingham, Alabama. Well, that was the last place I wanted to go because she was always talking about Jesus too much.

When I tried everything within my power and strength, I could not get up off the floor. I felt helpless and somewhat afraid. Things weren't looking up for me, so to speak. I gave up and told the Lord that if he restores my strength, I will go where he wanted me to go and say what he wanted me to say.

When I meant that in my heart, I felt the strength slowly restored in my body again, I started pulling myself up on the bed and I looked around. I was the only one in the bedroom, and my family did not know what I was going through.

Once my body became normal again, and the first opportunity or chance I had to visit my sister

Arquillia, I kept my word and went to Birmingham, Alabama, to visit her. Guess what the first thing she started talking about? It was Jesus. I knew not to turn a deaf ear to what she was saying because of my previous experience, begging Him for help. Prior to that point, I did not recognize him as my Savior. Her and a little 13-year-old girl led me to Jesus Christ by having me to repeat after them the sinner's prayer.

I asked the Lord to forgive me for my sins and missed deeds and to come into my heart and live with me. I started reading the *Bible* before I went to sleep at night. A bright light from Heaven shone on the word of God while I read John 15:1-27 and John 16:1-15 (NLT).

Jesus, the True Vine

15 *"I am the true grapevine, and my Father is the gardener. ² He cuts off every branch of mine that doesn't produce fruit, and he prunes the branches that do bear fruit so they will produce even more. ³ You have already been pruned and purified by the message I have given you. ⁴ Remain in me, and I will remain* *in you. For a branch cannot produce fruit if it is severed from the vine, and you cannot be fruitful unless you remain in me.*

[5] *"Yes, I am the vine; you are the branches. Those who remain in me, and I in them, will produce much fruit. For apart from me you can do nothing.* [6] *Anyone who does not remain in me is thrown away like a useless branch and withers. Such branches are gathered into a pile to be burned.* [7] *But if you remain in me and my words remain in you, you may ask for anything you want, and it will be granted!* [8] *When you produce much fruit, you are my true disciples. This brings great Glory to my Father.*

[9] *"I have loved you even as the Father has loved me. Remain in my love.* [10] *When you obey my commandments, you remain in my love, just as I obey my Father's commandments and remain in his love.* [11] *I have told you these things so that you will be filled with my joy. Yes, your joy will overflow!* [12] *This is my*

commandment: Love each other in the same way I have loved you. ¹³ *There is no greater love than to lay down one's life for one's friends.* ¹⁴ *You are my friends if you do what I command.* ¹⁵ *I no longer call you slaves, because a master doesn't confide in his slaves. Now you are my friends, since I have told you everything the Father told me.* ¹⁶ *You didn't choose me. I chose you. I appointed you to go and produce lasting fruit, so that the Father will give you whatever you ask for, using my name.* ¹⁷ *This is my command: Love each other.*

The World's Hatred

¹⁸ *"If the world hates you, remember that it hated me first.* ¹⁹ *The world would love you as one of its own if you belonged to it, but you are no longer part of the world. I chose you to come out of the world, so it hates you.* ²⁰ *Do you remember what I told you? 'A slave is not greater than the master.' Since they persecuted me, naturally they will persecute you. And if they*

had listened to me, they would listen to you. **21** They will do all this to you because of me, for they have rejected the one who sent me. **22** They would not be guilty if I had not come and spoken to them. But now they have no excuse for their sin. **23** Anyone who hates me also hates my Father. **24** If I hadn't done such miraculous signs among them that no one else could do, they would not be guilty. But as it is, they have seen everything I did, yet they still hate me and my Father. **25** This fulfills what is written in their Scriptures[a]: 'They hated me without cause.'

26 "But I will send you the Advocate[b]—the Spirit of truth. He will come to you from the Father and will testify all about me. **27** And you must also testify about me because you have been with me from the beginning of my ministry.

John 16:1-5 (NLT)

16 "I have told you these things so that you won't abandon your *faith.* [2] *For you will be expelled from the synagogues, and the time is coming when those who kill you will think they are doing a holy service for God.* [3] *This is because they have never known the Father or me.* [4] *Yes, I'm telling you these things now, so that when they happen, you will remember my warning. I didn't tell you earlier because I was going to be with you for a while longer.*

From that night forward, Jesus became my invisible friend, and he is my invisible friend today. Throughout this book, you will see God's faithfulness and how He helped to solve so many problems, and He will do the same for you, so let's really dig in and see some life-changing possibilities.

My Invisible Friend
and the Rottweiler Dog

One day I arrived early to work as usual, but suddenly, a big robust vicious Rottweiler came charging my way. The only thing I had in my hand was a small cellphone, which was no match for a one hundred pound plus vicious dog. My parents had always taught me not to run from a dog because that would cause the dog to attack me.

I immediately called my invisible friend, and he came to my rescue. He stopped the vicious dog from biting me. I was imagining that the dog could knock me down on the hard-concrete driveway and start biting me. Instead of me running from the vicious animal, I did the exact opposite. I ran after him for a few seconds after I realized that my invisible friend was a present help when I was in trouble. Later, I decided to go into the office.

Well, that was the highlight or topic of the day. Why? Because my coworkers saw my invisible friend come to my rescue by stopping the dog from biting me.

I began imagining that the dog was knocking me down on the hard-concrete driveway and biting me. I could have been unconscious from the fall and the bites. My coworkers would have to call an ambulance to take me to the hospital. I immediately imagined having plastic surgery, and my life never being the same again.

I took a deep breath during my random thoughts. I started thinking about when I met new people, they would ask what happened to your face? I am so happy that my invisible friend helped me when I was in trouble and stopped any harm that was coming my way. I noticed that my coworkers were too afraid to help. They just watched the entire situation or episode. Now, I feel so special to have a wonderful invisible friend that will always be with me.

My Invisible Friend and the
Poisonous Snake

On day two of my private journal, I would never forget that late afternoon when the sun was going down, and it was getting dark outside. I needed to go to the store to buy some food. I decided to go in my car, which was parked in the garage. I was going to the grocery store to get some milk, Kellogg's Frosted Flakes, bananas, and the list continued.

Just before I left, my invisible friend told me to turn on the outdoor lights at the front door of my house. Well, that did not make any sense to me. Why? Because I was driving my car and I would park it back in the garage. He reminded me again, and from experience, I knew my courageous friend was there to help me. With that thought in mind, I said, "Okay" and followed His instructions.

Immediately, when I came from the store and I parked in the garage, guess what I spotted in the garage? It was a big wasp flying around, and I refused to get out of my car. I backed the car out of the garage and parked it outside. That meant I had to walk to the front door to bring the groceries inside my house.

I was delighted that my invisible friend told me to leave the lights on at my front door. Why? Because as I was walking to the front door, I spotted a poisonous red, black, and yellow coral snake. I told the kids to stop, and they did immediately.

I thought, if that snake had a chance to bite me, my kids were too young to call for help or obtain assistance in this situation. I had the opportunity to pick up a big brick and throw it at the snake, and it went away.

I was so grateful that my invisible friend gave me a second chance by reminding me what He said about the front outdoor lights. I was also so thankful to get into my house safely after spotting a wasp and a poisonous snake that night.

Now, I am fully persuaded that my friend would neither leave me nor forsake me – EVER! Every morning I try to check in with my invisible friend to see what's on our schedule.

My Invisible Friend and the Anesthesia Drugs

N ow, let me tell you about day three when I was sick, and I had to see a doctor. When I went to my doctor, he said to me that he was going to do a blood test. I told him, "Why not," so he did, and the test results indicated that I had severe anemia.

The doctor had the nurse to call me at work to let me know that I needed to be hospitalized, and they needed to do surgery immediately.

"Well, sir, I cannot do that right away because I must find someone to keep my children during this process," I responded.

Once that was in place, I was well on my journey to the hospital to have surgery. I asked the nurse to check my weight before they gave me the anesthesia drugs. I wanted to make sure they were giving me the correct amount before surgery.

They gave me the drugs without weighing me because they used the information from my previous records. That weight was entirely wrong because I had lost weight since then. During the surgery, the doctors fixed the problem. When it was time for me to come back to life, the doctors were talking, and I could hear them. They were trying to bring me back, but I was given too much of the anesthesia drug.

My invisible friend came on the scene when I was in trouble again, and He used His mighty power to wake me up.

The doctors had been trying but were unsuccessful for the last thirty minutes. My invisible friend fixed the problem with His light touch, and I immediately woke up from the anesthesia. I was so happy and grateful to see my loved ones again because of the touch from my invisible friend.

A Battle with Cancer

During the surgery, it revealed that I had been dealing with cancer for ten long years before the doctors became aware of it. They were able to tell how long I had cancer by the different stages that they were looking at and how it had spread to the various lymph nodes in my body. My doctor found out that it was something severely wrong with me through the blood test.

I ended up staying in the hospital for three long weeks after the surgery. The most incredible part of my hospital stay was my invisible friend was hanging out with me. Even when I went home, He was there to talk with me and comfort me. I wrote several notebooks of information that He shared with me. It was so much fun until I hated it when I was well again because He seemed to have disappeared for a season.

My Invisible Friend Reaching Out to Help Others

I want to ask if you would like to meet my invisible friend too. Well, before that takes place, let me share some more information on how my invisible friend helped me to reach out to others. One day I had a one hundred dollar bill hidden in my dresser drawer, and he told me to give it to Jessica. I decided to call her and let her know that I had $100.00 to give her.

She was so touched by it because she needed some money to purchase some food for her children. Jessica said, "Thank you, so much."

She wanted to find out how did I knew the information about her needing some money. The truth was I did not know it at all, but I was following my invisible friend's instructions.

My Invisible Friend at Six Flags Over Texas

L et me tell you about another magnificent moment. When I was in Dallas at Six Flags over Texas, my two sons and their friends were having a blast riding the "Catwoman Whip." This particular ride would spin and tilt in a circular motion, building up speed as the ride whips around and upside down. Another ride they appeared to enjoy was the "Bugs Bunny Cloud Bouncer." This ride is where they had the opportunity to whirl through the sky over "Bugs Bunny Boomtown."

Well, after several rides as indicated above and much more, John developed a headache. When he told me about his headache, I decided to pass the information to my invisible friend. He instructed me to lay my hand on his head, and my invisible friend caused the headache to disappear. When that took place, John was happy again and ready to continue the fun that he was having at Six Flags.

How My Coworker Met My Invisible Friend

One day, my invisible friend led me to share the plan of salvation with a coworker. First, I asked him did he want to receive Jesus in his heart. He replied, "Yes," so at that point, I went to the next office to get his wife.

Once she was present, the three of us caught hands, and my invisible friend helped me to lead him in the plan of salvation. I asked him to repeat after me,

Dear Jesus, I ask you to forgive me of my sins and to come into my heart and live with me.

When he finished, he was so grateful to have a new life with Jesus. He kept telling me, "Thank you for sharing Jesus with me."

At the time, I was not aware that he only had one more day to live. He had been sick for a long time. When he came to work the next morning with his wife, I ran out of the meeting to greet them. I asked him if he was alright. He shook his head, "No" and that was the last time he was alive.

His wife called the ambulance, and they came immediately to his rescue. He was admitted to the hospital, but he did not survive. When it was time for his funeral, I asked my invisible friend "what am I going to say?" He wanted me to talk about his last "Golden Moments with Jesus."

I am still thankful to this day that my invisible friend allowed me to share the plan of salvation with my coworker, and I am looking forward to seeing him again in Heaven.

My Invisible Friend is Concerned About the Little Things in Life

As of today, I have noticed that my invisible friend is concerned about the little things in life as well as the significant hurdles in life. He demonstrated that He wants me to be happy and prepared for disappointments too. I know from experience that when His presence shows up that I need to get ready for something to happen. His presence showed up at 9:00 a.m.

I was getting out of my car and was going into the Dollar Store to purchase some liquid white-out. I asked the owner did they have any liquid white-out, and he assured me they did. With that thought in mind, I was happy for a few minutes, It took a few more minutes, and I was a little disappointed because they did not have the correct kind of white-out that I was expecting. They only had the dry paper strip kind. This meant that I needed to

go to a different location to find the liquid white-out. Instead of going back to a different store, I decided to go back to work, and my coworker decided to help me use her dry strip white-out, and things went very well.

My Invisible Friend Spared My Brother's Life

One day my invisible friend instructed me to go to Richmond, California and I was there for four days. I was praying and interceding for my brother to leave California. He was encouraged to leave just in time because a gunshot killed his best friend. They thought that they were killing my brother, but it was his best friend.

I am thankful to this day how the Lord has answered my prayer and spared his life. I did not know the young man or his family and my heart go out to them because his best friend's life could never be replaced.

A Trip to the Zoo

I came from a family of nine brothers and six sisters, and this episode was shared with me several times. My mother had to do a roll call to make sure that all of her children were present.

On that particular day, with so much excitement in the air, my mother did not follow her routine of counting her children before departure. Everyone headed to the New Orleans Zoo, which is a big thing for kids. Well, this took place when I was about two-years-old, and my entire family went on a field trip. I was left behind by mistake, and my family did not realize that I was missing until they returned home. They found me playing in a ditch, and my invisible friend was with me and protected me the whole time.

The Lord will preserve him and keep him alive (Psalm 41:2). This scripture is an indicator of how he preserved me and kept me alive from danger or harm.

A Bomb

I was told that one day I was playing under our frame house and found a red bomb. I thought it was another unusual gadget, and I immediately brought the item to my mother.

She looked at it, placed a phone call, and they left the house with the bomb. Shortly after they got to the woods to dispose the bomb, it went off. This was another incident where my invisible friend saved our entire family from being destroyed.

Psalm 32:7 - *You shall preserve me from trouble; You shall surround me with songs of deliverance.*

I am so thankful to the Lord for how he has protected us from trouble and kept us alive and well.

A Teaching Position

When I first moved to Texas, I lived with one of my brothers. Well, after being there for several months, he received orders to go to Korea. In the meantime, I prayed and believed God would deliver me a teaching position. Why? Because I needed this job so I could continue and live in Texas. I needed money for an apartment, food, and a car to even go to an interview.

Immediately after I had the opportunity to purchase my first car, I completed the interview with the school district in Copperas Cove, Texas. I told my family and friends that I know I have the job. The Lord knows that the job is mine, but the school needed to realize it and give me a phone call. I was so excited when I received that wonderful phone call within a week that I had the teaching position.

I went to the school, and they showed me my classroom, but I had no students to teach. I was on payroll for a whole month, and they decided to gather some students from other teachers so I could have some students to teach. I looked at the situation and said that it was another creative miracle that God performed for me, and I have been teaching school for the last thirty-seven years in different locations.

> *Philippians 4:19* *And my God shall supply all your need according to His riches in Glory by Christ Jesus.*

Meeting My Husband

Well, years ago, I wanted to get married, and I believed God that he had told me that I was going to meet my husband to be before October was over. I usually attend church for the 10:00 a.m., Sunday morning service only. My excuse was that I needed to get ready for work by preparing my lesson plan and activities to teach my classroom students on Monday and the rest of the week. I was thinking that this was the very last Sunday of the month, and I had to attend church service that Sunday night at 7:00 p.m. only to meet my future husband.

I was looking for the guy that my friend had shown me in a dream. The pastor of the church told him to stick his head out from the sound booth to greet the congregation. When he did, I immediately noticed that he was the guy that I had seen in the dream, and I had heard some good talk about him. The talk was from my invisible friend, and he let me know that he was going to be my husband.

I went around asking different people, "Did they know the guy in the sound booth?"

I finally found one person in the church that knew him, and she introduced him to me. He got my phone number and called me that same night to talk, and he let me know that the Lord showed him a vision that I was to be his wife.

To make a long story short, he had a military order and had to leave for a few weeks. While he was gone, he called me on the phone and proposed to me. He asked me would I be his wife, and I said "Yes," and within a month and two weeks, we were married.

From that marriage, we had two wonderful sons, and we inherited one son who made a total of three sons.

I am so grateful that my invisible friend allowed me to be with my husband for thirty-three wonderful years, five months, eighteen days, nine hours, and twenty-eight minutes together. Truly, he was a man of God after his own heart, and Christ had been the center and circumference of our marriage.

I had the opportunity to experience God's very best through him. He has made a mark in our lives that can never be erased, in the lives of our children, grandchildren, family, and many friends.

These are some of the comments that his sons have made. His first son was named Daniel Perry, and he said, "Dad, I want to say thank you for being who you are. Thank you for making me who I am. You are the best."

Marcus Perry, the second son, stated that, "I know you're in Heaven now, but please know this is true, that everything I am today is all because of you. Not a day passes by, Dad, that you don't cross my mind. I will always love you. You're in Glory with Christ, leaving earthly things behind. I can't wait to see you again; this I know is true. Thank you for being a faithful father."

Michael Rivera, the third son's comments, "Dad, you are the example I look to when it comes to being a husband, father, and follower of Christ. What you have done for my life is something I will cherish and hold onto for the rest of my life.

Before my husband went to be with the Lord, he told me, "No man can come into this world or leave out without God's Permission."

Truly, my husband was a man of God after his own heart.

Acts 13:22. *Jesse in the Bible was a man after God's own heart too, for he did everything God wanted him to do.*

Prayer Changes Things

One day the Lord gave me an unction to pray for my niece, and her name is Miracle. He let me know that if I pray, he will spare her life. At that moment, I was unaware of what the child and parents were experiencing at the time. I shared with the parents that God had directed me to pray for your child daily. She said, "Thank you," and immediately, tears started coming from her eyes.

She stated that her daughter had died in her arms. God brought her back alive, and I know that it was a serious miracle of God. This was another episode of God's mighty power.

In the book of Hebrews 4:16, indicated this would come one day.

Hebrews 4:16 - *"Let us therefore come boldly unto the throne of grace, that we may obtain mercy, and find grace to help in time of need.*

Riding Home

I can recall when I was riding with my brother Mitchell because I could not drive. My wonderful friend was letting me know to tell my brother to go in a different direction. I told him to please do not go this way, and he said, "Old girl, I know what I am doing."

To make a long story short, he drove a little farther and guess what happened because he did not listen to my friend indeed? A car came along and drove us off the highway, and we had an accident. I said, "Mitchell, I tried to tell you, but you did not listen, and now what?

The answer is in the Bible.

Proverbs 3:5-6 *"Trust in the Lord with all your heart; do not depend on your own understanding. Seek his will in all you do,* *and he will direct your paths."* (New Living Translation)

My Twin Sister

O ne day my twin sister, Sarah, shared her heart with me concerning the trouble she has had with transportation. She is a person that puts the Lord first in her life, and her second job is a professional domestic worker. Well, she needed a dependable vehicle to run errands, attend church, and to go back and forth to work.

Sarah had mentioned that the Lord had revealed to her that a particular person would buy her a car. She told the individual, but she was not about to do a thing like that with her money.

Not only that but, Pastor Rosia Duncan prophesied that someone would buy her a new car. Sarah had waited for years, telling different people that God said that someone was going to buy her a brand-new car. Some people she shared the information with thought she had lost her mind, others said, "Are you sure?"

"In this day in time, you mean that someone is going to buy you a brand-new car, I can see a used one. People need to make every penny count, and why do you think someone is going to do that for you just because you think that God said it?"

Sarah continued to be strong in her faith, and she took God at His word. Sarah and I discussed a plan in detail, and we thought about getting a vehicle for $4,000 in the meantime. When we went to Pastor Rosia Duncan's church, she prophesied to us that I had something to do with getting the brand-new SUV vehicle for my twin sister. When she said that, my twin sister, and I looked at each other in shock, and she immediately started praising God and flail out on the floor. She did not know that I had told the Lord that if it is His Will for me to get the car for my twin sister, please, have Pastor Duncan to speak it.

Once she spoke it, that was the confirmation that I needed to hear and know that it was the Lord's purpose and plan. I said, "Lord, you can count it as done because the best thing that I can do is to obey you with joy in my heart."

1 Corinthians 10:26 *For the earth is the Lord's and everything in it.*

Once my son, Daniel, and I drove back to Texas, I went to a car dealer that same day. I let them know that I was looking for a small SUV for my twin sister, and they had one on the lot. God blessed me to get the car that same day. When I gave her the car, she immediately started praising the Lord for how He had brought his word to pass. I had to laugh because I was so thankful for what the Lord had done.

Sarah stated, "Faith is not what you see, but it is what you believe. When you ask God for something in faith, you must believe, and you shall receive it because he is a miracle worker."

> **Hebrews 11:6** *But without faith it is impossible to please him: for he that cometh to God must believe that he is, and that he is a rewarder of them that diligently seek him.*

Next, God was honoring His word.

> **Philippians 4:19** - *But my God shall supply all your need according to his riches in Glory by Christ Jesus. The car was a serious need for Sarah on so many levels and he supplied it.*

Philippians 4:19 - *"And this same God who takes care of me will supply all your needs from his glorious riches, which have given to us in Christ Jesus. Now Glory be to God our Father forever and ever. Amen.*

My Best Friend

One day I was at my best friend's house, and she let me know that she would like to have this particular space for an office. She went on to say how much it would cost, and she had plans to complete the project much later.

I thought this is one plan that needed to be done immediately. Because of the phone calls and business, she needed a space in her home without any distractions. I told her to just start speaking it and believe God for her office to be done. When I shared the information, I did not know that God was going to use me to finance the office. When God shared that with me, I looked around to see if he was talking to someone else. Then, I realized that I was on the hot seat again to take care of

God's mission. I shared it with my best friend, and she said, "Are you sure?"

I said, "Yes, and you can have your daughter to get the construction worker to set a time when he can come over to fix your office."

My best friend has been giving God all the honor and praise for what He had done. She said that she had desired to have an office for years at her house, especially with French doors.

Psalm 37:4 *Take delight in the Lord, and he will give you your heart's desires.*

Never Give Up on Your Child

Why? because God never gives up on us. He is patient and long-suffering. I was told that when I was a toddler, I did not start walking until I was almost three years old. My twin sister was walking and saying things. My family members had to carry me where ever I went. Not only that, they told me repeatedly that I had trouble talking. It would take me five minutes to say one word because I had a profound stuttering problem. No one would listen to what I had to say because it took too long for me to get my words out. Some people told my mother just to slap me with a dirty dishrag, and that would make me talk. During those days, we did not have speech therapists as they do now.

When I became school-age, life did not become any better, but worse. My twin sister and I started in the same grade, but she was smart, and I was the opposite.

The first year I failed, they held my twin sister behind, trying to keep us together. Once I had a habit of not performing in school, my twin sister passed me up, and she graduated from high school before I did.

My younger sister Virginia caught up with me. She understood her math and any other assignments better than I did. She had to help me many times. My report card had so many "F's" until I thought that it was good. I found out that it was terrible when I showed my report card to my mother. She bragged on all the other children report cards, but when she saw mine, she said, "Please go and get a switch."

Years ago, A switch is a small tree limb that was twisted together that you broke off a tree. My mother would tear my little legs up because of the bad grades I brought home every six weeks.

My reading skills, comprehension, or ability to recall facts were just bad. I can recall when my mother would tell me a word, and when I saw that same word, later on, I could not remember it to save my life. I think because I knew that the switch was waiting for my legs.

Reading, talking, walking, and explaining myself was a devasting part of my life. My family members did not expect me to finish high school, but when I look back over my life today, my faithful friend has made the difference that I needed in life to be successful. I am so thankful that I am a retired school teacher and I could not give up on any of my students because of our God did not give up on me.

My Economics Class

I can recall when I was in the eighth grade, and my Economics teacher just gave up on me. She became so distraught that she took my report card out of her desk in front of the entire class and gave me "F's" for the remaining six-weeks and the semester.

Once that episode took place, I did not need to work hard any longer for the remainder of the year. At that time, I was working on making a dress, and it happened to be brown. My mother bought me one spool of thread, and it did not last long.

As you can recall, I came from a large family and buying things was like a needle in the haystack that you were looking for. With that thought in mind, I was asking to borrow thread from different classmates to finish sewing my dress.

Once I was finished, my teacher pointed out that I had used too many different color threads to complete my project. I had brown, pink, blue, green, yellow, and any other color that I could borrow. The dress that I had completed was beautiful only in my eyes. When my Economics Teacher graded it, she looked at me and added to my collections of "F's."

This was another time that my invisible friend had to comfort me because I was too through with that teacher and class. With all the negative experiences that I have had in school, it taught me a lesson -- never give up on your students and always encourage them because you may not know their economic background, living conditions, and their emotional state.

I will always remember that my school district had a motto for us to follow, and it was to "Teach so that students learn to their maximum potential." This phrase was always inspirational to me and comforting.

Psalm 86:17 - *Indicated that Because You, Lord, have helped me and comforted me.*

Meeting My Invisible Friend

If you need anything, I would love for you to meet my supernatural friend, and His name is Jesus. You can ask Him to come into your heart and live with you. He will never leave you or forsake you. Jesus will be your wonderful friend throughout life and then in eternity. He will supply your every need according to his riches in Glory by Christ Jesus.

All the previous information is about my invisible friend that is living on the inside of me, which is Jesus. I asked Him to forgive me for my sins and to come into my heart and live with me. It was just that simple, and He has been living with me ever since.

Romans 10:9-10 - *If you confess with your mouth, 'Jesus is Lord, and believe in your heart*

*that God raised Him from the dead, you will be
saved. For it is with your heart that you believe
and are justified, and it is with your mouth that
you confess and are saved.'*

I have included these scripture verses again as a
reminder that Jesus is the true vine according to
John 15:1 – John 16:15 (NLT).

Jesus, the True Vine

15 *"I am the true grapevine, and my
Father is the gardener. ² He cuts off
every branch of mine that doesn't
produce fruit, and he prunes the
branches that do bear fruit so they will
produce even more. ³ You have
already been pruned and purified by
the message I have given
you. ⁴ Remain in me, and I will remain
in you. For a branch cannot produce
fruit if it is severed from the vine, and
you cannot be fruitful unless you
remain in me.*

*⁵ "Yes, I am the vine; you are the
branches. Those who remain in me,
and I in them, will produce much fruit.
For apart from me you can do*

nothing. [6] Anyone who does not remain in me is thrown away like a useless branch and withers. Such

branches are gathered into a pile to be burned. [7] But if you remain in me and my words remain in you, you may ask for anything you want, and it will be granted! [8] When you produce much fruit, you are my true disciples. This brings great Glory to my Father.

[9] "I have loved you even as the Father has loved me. Remain in my love. [10] When you obey my commandments, you remain in my love, just as I obey my Father's commandments and remain in his love. [11] I have told you these things so that you will be filled with my joy. Yes, your joy will overflow! [12] This is my commandment: Love each other in the same way I have loved you. [13] There is no greater love than to lay down one's life for one's friends. [14] You are my friends if you do what I command. [15] I no longer call you slaves, because a master doesn't confide in his slaves. Now you are my

friends, since I have told you everything the Father told me. ¹⁶ You

didn't choose me. I chose you. I appointed you to go and produce lasting fruit, so that the Father will give you whatever you ask for, using my name. ¹⁷ This is my command: Love each other.

The World's Hatred

¹⁸ "If the world hates you, remember that it hated me first. ¹⁹ The world would love you as one of its own if you belonged to it, but you are no longer part of the world. I chose you to come out of the world, so it hates you. ²⁰ Do you remember what I told you? 'A slave is not greater than the master.' Since they persecuted me, naturally they will persecute you. And if they had listened to me, they would listen to you. ²¹ They will do all this to you because of me, for they have rejected the one who sent me. ²² They would not be guilty if I had not come and spoken to them. But now they have no excuse for their sin. ²³ Anyone who

hates me also hates my Father. ²⁴ If I hadn't done such miraculous signs among them that no one else could do, they would not be guilty. But as it is, they have seen everything I did, yet they still hate me and my Father. ²⁵ This fulfills what is written in their Scriptures[a]: 'They hated me without cause.'

²⁶ "But I will send you the Advocate— the Spirit of truth. He will come to you from the Father and will testify all about me. ²⁷ And you must also testify about me because you have been with me from the beginning of my ministry.

John 16:1-5 (NLT)

16 "I have told you these things so that you won't abandon your faith. ² For you will be expelled from the synagogues, and the time is coming when those who kill you will think they are doing a holy service for God. ³ This is because they have never known the Father or me. ⁴ Yes, I'm telling you these things now, so that when they happen, you will remember my warning. I didn't tell you earlier because I was going to be with you for a while longer.

Once I finished reading the above scripture, it left a one-time magnificent experience. I guess I needed that, but do not feel left out if it does not happen to you because we are all different. The main thing is to confess Jesus Christ as your Savior and Lord and to give Him control of your life. The next step is to connect with a church where Jesus is Lord and King and to continue your relationship with Jesus. With that thought in mind, He will lead and guide you as you acknowledge Him in all your ways. Know that you have dual citizenship, one on earth and Heaven.

Luke 22-29 - *And I confer on you a kingdom, just as my Father conferred one on me.*

About the Author

Mary Perry has a Master of Science Degree in Education. She is a mother, evangelist, widow, and retired teacher who worked with the Blind and Visually Impaired from birth to 22 years of age in the Central Texas area for over 38 years. Mary Perry is trying to reach individuals during the COVID-19 Pandemic to let them know there is hope in these challenging times of home confinement. Mary Perry's debut book is a must-read for those who have a desire to experience a supernatural change in their life.

Resources

Scripture quotations marked NLT are from the Holy Bible: New Living Translation. 1997 by Tyndale House Publishers, Inc. Wheaton, Illinois

Scripture quotations marked KJV are from the Holy Bible: The Original King James Version. 1985 by Dugan Publishers, Inc. Gordonsville, Tennessee 38563

Contact Information

Mary Perry

415 E FM 2410 Rd, #2088
Harker Heights, Texas 76548
Email: wmperry2006@yahoo.com

MY TRUE INVISIBLE FRIEND

www.ingramcontent.com/pod-product-compliance
Lightning Source LLC
Chambersburg PA
CBHW021222020426
42331CB00003B/424